T0168309

THE

WORD

WE

USED

FOR

IT

WISCONSIN POETRY SERIES

Ronald Wallace, *Series Editor*

THE

WORD

WE

USED

FOR

IT

MAX GARLAND

THE UNIVERSITY OF WISCONSIN PRESS

The University of Wisconsin Press
1930 Monroe Street, 3rd Floor
Madison, Wisconsin 53711-2059
uwpress.wisc.edu

3 Henrietta Street, Covent Garden
London WC2E 8LU, United Kingdom
eurospanbookstore.com

Printed in the United States of America

This book may be available in a digital edition.

Library of Congress Cataloging-in-Publication Data
Names: Garland, Max, 1950– author.
Title: The word we used for it / Max Garland.
Other titles: Wisconsin poetry series.
Description: Madison, Wisconsin : The University of Wisconsin Press,
    [2017] | Series: Wisconsin poetry series
Identifiers: LCCN 2017015525 | ISBN 9780299314347 (pbk. : alk. paper)
Subjects: | LCGFT: Poetry.
Classification: LCC PS3557.A7162 W67 2017 | DDC 811/.54—dc23
LC record available at https://lccn.loc.gov/2017015525

for Sam Bowling

1939–2016

Living is no laughing matter:
   You must live your life with great seriousness
   like a squirrel, for example—

   —Nazim Hikmet, "On Living"

CONTENTS

Sway   3

I

At the Opening of an Exhibition   7

Hymn for Joseph   12

Sciurus Carolinesis   14

Grit   16

Joy   17

The Word We Used for It   18

The Woman Who Waved from the River   19

If a Man Had a Boat   21

Rehabilitation   22

Mega-Foods   23

Keep in Touch   24

Bat in the House   25

A Photograph of Earth from Space, 1972   27

II

Orion Spur   33

Heaven   34

Chesterfield   35

Ghost Army   36

The Bees   40

Hollyhocks   41

Green Day   42

Nightly News   43

Get Right With God   44

I Call Your Name   45

When I Think of You I Think of Her   47

Stay   48

Spring Snow   49

III

Search Committee   53

Reception   55

Jesus Jogs   57

If You Really Had To   59

Happiness   60

Tupelo   61

After Leaving *The Poetics of Space* on a
Chair on the Deck All Night   63

The World as You Saw It   65

The Wren   66

Snowflake   67

Chickadees   69

Home   70

Blink   71

The Best Things in Life Are the Most Expensive 74

ACKNOWLEDGMENTS

I'm grateful to the editors of the following publications in which some of these poems first appeared—

Arts and Letters: "The Woman Who Waved from the River," "Snowflake."

Folio: "Blink."

Gettysburg Review: "Bat in the House," "Hymn for Joseph," "Chickadees."

New England Review: "Grit," "Get Right With God."

Prairie Schooner: "Hollyhocks."

Subtropics: "Sciurus Carolinesis," "The Word We Used for It."

Volume One: "Mega-Foods," "Rehabilitation."

THE

WORD

WE

USED

FOR

IT

SWAY

Many nights it held us aloft.
We knew each other's weight as surely
as we knew each other's lightness.

Hips sway, branches, boats, the surface
of earth sways according to the instruments
and frequency of the hills—everything

made of waves—light, pulse,
low vowels not quite risen to the level
of human speech.

The swirls of the fingertips
seem the track of some old swaying.
It held us many nights aloft.

Took the shape of us as its own—
sometimes rivers and hills, some nights
wind through the long wet grass.

I

AT THE OPENING OF AN EXHIBITION

"Offering of the Angels": paintings from the Uffizi Gallery

Jesus flies from frame to frame. Here
he's an infant with an ancient face.
And here he's already risen, or hasn't been born,
or hovers in Limbo
with hordes of the half-lost below him.

The gallery goers can never quite catch
the spirit in flight. It tends to blur
at the edge of human vision. Millions
of rods and cones in the retina,
and still by the time we focus
it's tucked back under these strokes
of post-Renaissance paint.

By the time we turn it's limp on the cross.
Crowned in the air. Cultural artifact.
Money in the bank.

Maybe *once*? I saw the pigment slightly tremble.
It's the rods, right? that scan the periphery
for motion, while the cones go for the meat
of the matter, suckers for the obvious.

All I know about looking at art
is that it takes a lot of movement
to keep a painting still. Like watching
the beat of a hummingbird's wings.
You know it's happening, but all you see
is iridescence poised, posed at the lip
of some flower of this world.

All you see is the lovely hover.

The flight itself dissolves, reassembles always
one crucial instant quicker than the eye.
What I feel is the *implication* of wing beats
in these paintings, this town, this night.

Or maybe it's just the rush and buzz
of the complimentary wine I feel
as we browse madonnas and mangers
and martyrs nearly four hundred years
after the last drop of paint dried.

As we stand in our glamorous shoes,
and muted layers, garments
so miraculously soft
the children who spun them
might as well have been the angels
in these paintings, just as anonymous
and poorly paid.

All I know is that it's the whirling
that composes the fixed, right?
Some everlasting motion
that steadies the temporal.

But it's strange, the face that strikes me most
tonight is not an angel's, nor the Lord's,
nor God's tired-ahead-of-time face
as he triggers the pulse in Adam.

It's a face in a painting by Giovanni Martinelli.
Ecce Homo—Behold the Man, is the title.
It's only hours before the crucifixion.
Pilate presents the beaten Lord to the rabble,
duly agitated. Jesus stands, unsteady,
already crowned with thorns.

They always like to rough-up gods
a few crucial centuries
before they stamp them on the coins.

But it's this young woman with an infant in her arms,
who gets much of the light in the painting
as Jesus looks down from the balcony.

Elsewhere in the museum—there's a pregnant virgin
in a flame-red party dress. There's baby John
and baby Jesus. Flakes of manna falling
from the blue vault of heaven.

Behold the Man is the title, but it's the woman
we mostly behold. *Ecce Femina?*
She seems familiar, though likely she's a model
picked up cheap from the streets of Florence
back in a cruel time, as all times are,
to hold the future in her face.
It's a long way from then until this night.
It's partly that *time* we've come here to feel.
And these ancient strokes of paint
time seems to faintly animate.

What is it about the nameless dead
that won't quite fully fall down?
Why be haunted by the ghost of this girl
looking up at the man they've tried their best
to beat the god out of?

Is she *offering* her infant? Holding the child up
for some last ditch blessing? And which way
would such a blessing flow?

Sometimes I still think the lie of art is *not*.
Sometimes I think a spirit moves
in the particulars of a painting
like they say the molecules move
to give the illusion of solid walls, floor,
the physical bodies in this gallery.

For me, the least dead thing in the room
is the stroke of light in this girl's face
that won't go out, or how young
old art can seem, or how far the painter
saw beyond what he intended.

Sadness inhabits this canvas, incurable,
except for the woman's face, caught right
at the brink of—*adoration?* That's the word,
I think. But not *for* this man, or god. I mean

adoration *is* the god. Not the one adored.
Not the man *beheld*. I mean *beholding*
is the god, the brief embrace of now,
blur at the edge of the retina's reach
out where the cones can't see, but the rods
sense faint unearthly motion.

It's the implication of wings, like waves
that catch and let go, like the bristles
of Martinelli's brush caught
and lifted and left these strokes of light
on a woman and child, and therefore magnified
the darkness, and therefore the intervening years.
It's the *looking*, not the icon observed.

What is truth? Pilate asked Jesus
just before the scene in this painting.
The rabble was already assembled,
ready for blood. For all I know,
I might have been among them.

Wine hums in my head. A woman's heels
click on a staircase. In my pocket,
God climbs from the surfaces of coins.

Truth? According to the record,
there was no answer. Except
for the looking that lights her face.
What flies from frame to frame.
What's crucified when nothing is adored.
How the *holy* in this painting moves
from the woman *to* the Lord.

HYMN FOR JOSEPH

The choir sang "Blessed Assurance"
with a rhythm like sawing a board.
Mary sat in the stain of the window,
a shard of God
in the crook of her shawl.

There were foretastes of glory,
Magi in the backfield—
grave-faced, lovestruck.

And *Joseph?*—where he always stood—
out of frame, out of mind,
brushing barn lint from his sleeve,
trying to look *related.*

They should have more hymns for Joseph,
compose a childhood
of better choirs in general.

Ever notice how "Blessed Assurance"
speeded up
sounds a lot like "Zip-a-Dee-Doo-Dah"?

I remember a portrait of Jesus
where you could see his heart
like a ripe pepper in his chest.

But who could ever pluck it out?

Not Mary, with her swan neck
and opaque fingers. Not Joseph,
poor man of such sorrows,
and downwelling spirit.

They should construct a faith
with slightly fewer wings than this,
an altar made of straw,
a Joseph who really gets the girl,
a Jesus in his father's shop—

tapping and planing, everything
by hand—here's a bed he made,
a wagon tongue, a window frame.

Busy little Jesus. Saint Joseph
of the sawdust—fragrant,
billowing. Mary in the night.

SCIURUS CAROLINESIS

It's hopeless how she loves this life.
The gray squirrel digs a small moon's
worth of craters in the yard.
Some she fills, some leaves open.
I've seen her work a walnut, still green,
round and round, shaving the surface
down to the meat. It moves in her claws
like a planet, or a bead
bigger and quicker than worry.
By love, I mean she uses the day
down to the last morsel of light—digs, barks,
insults the crow, wields
and lashes her tail like a glorified whip.
There's a charge in her, wild volts.
A livid motion, leaping from red pine
to hackberry, the single forepaw catching first,
swinging under, then over, then onto
the branch. She's a circus
when she takes to the power lines,
racing the live wire above the lowly
addresses. She's a spiral of serious sleep
in the high hollow of the pin oak.
By love, I mean filling herself
with small right intentions. By life,
I mean she looks at you from the railings.
A kind of dare is in her, her tail curled
like a bass clef, or mutant fern.
You won't catch her. She's scrolling
from scent to sound to slightest motion.
However the light moves
might be ruin, or rich enough to rob.

The way she ransacks, hoards, loses,
lashes, bluffs the crouched cat,
the unleashed dog, her death,
a dozen times a day, is what I mean
by hopeless how she loves this life.

GRIT

The light, half crippled from the cold, nevertheless limps into town.
The leafless trees and shrubs seem like stragglers from a dream
I can only remember the ragged edges of, something
about breath being hard to come by, and a rip in the landscape
or across the skin. There's week-old snow on the fields,
sheet metal sky, the neighboring roofs all bristle backed,
thin ridges of white where the shingles overlap.
A week's worth of tracks on the lawn have frozen over
and over—paw prints, claw prints intersect, crisscross,
loop around the spirea and lilac. I used to believe
I'd find words, a truth some day in those tracks
and backtracks. The gray squirrel would intertwine
his path with the rabbit. The crow would bound among
the scrawl, and by noon the loops and staggered shapes
in snow would read—*God is a sunflower seed,*
or *Behold the buried walnut, the apple core,* or
Scattered before us lies the bounty of bread crust.
But I never read that—just broken snow,
scratchings, small purposeful trails punctuated
by quick sidesteps, leaps, soft landings.
This morning light, though metallic
and without warmth, has come a long way
to register the particulars. I shouldn't complain.
Ninety-four million miles from hydrogen to here—
wave, particle, photon, field. The trees scrounge
their shapes from memory and the deep predictions
of roots outwanting the starkness. So do I, scrounge
through snow and dream and shape of day
for something to be or say worth half the grit
it took the gray light to get here, or the squirrel
to bound into the frozen morning after morning
and dig his living out.

JOY

Just to know how it felt I stood under the red pine.
It was 10 below and the sun was not quite up
and the moon not quite down, and the air so cold

you couldn't call it cold anymore, but sort of comical
on the intake, and the lungs were like—*Are you serious?*
The small three-pronged tracks in the snow

belonged to creatures no longer of this earth.
The paw prints, as well, were the only traces
of what we once called *rabbits* when such things

bounded from the shrubberies. And the light
which began to climb over the rim of horizon
appeared stunned like ancestors in old photographs

seem stunned. You look at them in their suspenders
and bonnets and the austerity of their faces
as if they knew, even then, in the minute's wait

for the shutter to close, they were goners. As if they
knew the reason for the picture was time without pity. So
I stood under the red pine, took a few more breaths

from deep in the glacial instant of my one and only life,
which hurt a little, like joy, by which I mean the edge of joy
where it sharpens itself for the work it has to do.

THE WORD WE USED FOR IT

It's trying to snow, my mother said. *It's* coming up a storm.
But *it* wasn't the weather, nor the day, nor wind. *It*
exerted effort, and had will—cold will, ill will,
or fine bright will—*It's* clearing up, she'd say.

God wasn't *it*, exactly, nor was the Devil, though *it*
might rain like the dickens, which meant the Devil,
and *it* was hot as hell in mid-July. We were blasted about
by *it*. Bore the brunt, at times, or were at times

passed over, thank the Lord, by the worst of *it*.
It's morning, she'd almost sing. *It's* day. And then
of course, *it's* getting dark, and dark was *it*
all night except for the burning of dreams

though *it* was in the dreams sometimes,
a bit of the burning *it*self. *It* was time,
but bigger than time. Time was only
how you tracked *it*, briefly pinned *it* down.

It's noon, we might say. Or soon, or over.
But *it* was never really over. Beyond the river and leaves,
under the wells, from back in the throat
you could feel the vibration, as *it*

moved to the top of the mouth. Then flicked
by the tongue through the teeth—*it*
rode out into the world, but wasn't the world, nor
the voice, nor even remotely the word we used for *it*.

THE WOMAN WHO WAVED FROM THE RIVER

I think there was a circus. It's bad
when the people die who could tell you.
I remember dust and torn paper
where they put the tent, stamped grass
and leftover scrapings. The animals
are mixed with storybook beasts
and dreams. The animals might not
have exactly existed. In those days
we were easily amazed. Flagpole sitters,
iron bar benders, men who buried themselves
three days in a vault. You could call them
and talk on the radio. *How does it feel?*
you could ask. Sky jumpers. Water-ski shows
where the women wore Catalinas
and sped downriver forever. The small
wet woman at the top of the pyramid
once waved to me, I believe. The people
who could verify, that's what I miss.
Did the skywriter trace the name
of our town, or the verse in the Bible
that would save our souls? Did he
parachute down onto the car lot?
Instead of a plane was it a gull
that banked, then broke into glitter
girls wore in their hair that summer?
They die with the details, the people
who could tell you, snug in the pockets
of the suits they were saving, in the creases
of dresses, in the cup of shadow under their hands.
Powdery hands. Dust and scrapings, blown paper.

How could there have been a circus
with no animals? And the woman who waved to me
from the river, all the way out of sight?
She must have seen everything,
up in her pyramid—treeline, skyline, spectral
shore. Every year, for the sake of the dead,
I believe in her a little more.

IF A MAN HAD A BOAT

My father believed if a man had a boat,
given the length of the river, and the brevity
of life, and given the milk route he rose
to run each morning with the moon
still out as he slipped from the trailer
over the blue gravel, and lifted all day
the cases of sweetmilk and buttermilk,
and stocked the grocery coolers,
and charmed the cashiers, and given
the memory of his own father drunk
and dripping from the river, the car
down deep, and his mother sharpening
on the piano her powers of forgiveness,
the war barely over, and given the wide
green of the Ohio with its coal barges and tugs,
and the weight of the current and the gulls
like little gods, a man with a boat might ride
things out, glide above the tangle and muck,
feel a better brand of wind, and smell the rich rot
of silt along the banks, and given the light
burnished surface, all silver and living, and day
bright as bracelets, if he could just buy a boat
all waters were his, and where they led—
some glittering sandbar with women in Catalinas
like Esther Williams, and no more cold half-
dollar's worth of moon to wake up under,
nor sour rubbery smell of milk and refrigerant,
if a man had a boat, there'd be time and light
and wind, and one hand over the side just
skimming up spray.

REHABILITATION

312A has a broken arm though sometimes
it's her leg. Bed 312B has lost her Kleenex
and given name. The loss leaks out

into the summer grass which doesn't know
it's green, under the sun which is slowly
turning to iron. Nevertheless, it's day.

312A was named for a movie star her mother
loved. Occasionally 312B is her own mother
and sometimes she's married to a dream

in which she's fallen from everywhere
and landed in a tree. *How
will we ever get down from here?*

she asks me. I tell her we're not in a tree.
I'm a professional liar. I tell her we'll be fine.
The sun will continue for as long as it can.

Maybe once we *were* in a tree, but now
we're just down the hall from flocks
of nurses wearing flowers. We shall not want.

Need not toil. Sometimes I'm her son,
and sometimes her boyfriend in heaven.
Here's a red button to push and nurses

will fly down from their stations.
It's fine not to be in a tree anymore.
Look, if I raise the blinds how the grass

minds its own business, low and safe,
exactly the color we need it to be.

MEGA-FOODS

The sky is so muscular it's nobody's business
where the sun went or why. Who wants to know?
A ripped, gray marbled, low-riding bruiser of a sky.
It's in no mood. Your best bet is to stand
in the parking lot of Mega-Foods
as if on the brink of leaving. Fondle your car keys
like a rosary, or a young snake's rattle. Maybe

as if on the brink of leaving is the presiding angel
of days like this, and asphalt is her blessing.
It won't quite rain, nor indicate clearing.
Clouds ride the rooftops like stolen horses.
In fact, there's a hint of gunplay on the wind,

though maybe that's just me. It's a good day
for not taking stock of your life. Hawks
first learned to hover over the blood-
streaked highways on days such as this.
A sheet of newspaper pins itself against the hubcap
of a parked car like an exiled fortune
wanting back in its cookie. *Don't push it*
some voice in the brain bristles, though
later it will seem the sky itself has spoken.

KEEP IN TOUCH

The gulls glide in and out of heaven,
though each time they swallow the key.
It's hard to get in by merely looking.

Every year a little more I believed
has settled to the bottom, silt of faith
down where the catfish stir.

Young as I was, evidence flashed
cheap as minnows. Beetles and striders
walked right across the surface.

I prayed to the beard of Moses in the clouds.
Every dove was slightly Jesus. Every
meadowlark's breast was Mary's own.

It's strange to lose a thing the size of a god
but not his blessings. Like no hard feelings.

You knock—and only knuckle bones.
You seek—and only glitter falls
like the light on this river.

Bee balm, milkweed, canary grass
move in the afternoon wind. Blue sky,
keep in touch.

BAT IN THE HOUSE

What you hear in sleep is the swim of live leather
as the bat sweeps over your face on the pillow,
takes his laps around the room,
at each turn unravels
a little more than you dreamed
until the last thread is fear
and there you are.

Consider the naked skin, how much it takes
to reach the lamp, eyeglasses, the last shirt
thrown down.

Consider a bracelet of bat, a livid tattoo.
Consider the strangeness
of sixty squeaks per second
bouncing back from your body.

You've gone into this before.
You've read how clean they are,
how well they hear the shape of a thing,
how little harm they mean.

You've tried to outfox fear with learning,
but the chemical self is newborn each night.
The bedtime heart is the world's worst student.

Later, when you've managed it, wielded
the fish net and broom, heard the screechings
of the tangled creature, counted the bared,
tiny beautiful teeth
and coaxed the bat to freedom,
you feel humane, but unconsoled.

Every wink of the curtain, every wind has life.
Chiroptera is the name of the order, *flying hand*.
And the night seems one thick flock
between the blotted moon and where

you lie and close your eyes
and try not to know, but know
your brother, flying blind—

squinch-face, baby-tooth—
much easier to save than love,
will come again in sleep.

A PHOTOGRAPH OF EARTH FROM SPACE, 1972

If light shone on this rock long
if somehow the outcast atoms
shed their solitary natures   tinkered
with embracing
laddered into molecules
and water washed around

it was only a matter of time
until time   urged forward
all this   and us
as if it needed someone

to tend the garden of numbers
as if the planet wanted watching
and so launched forth
some aspiration upward

and then came prophecy
and history
and a good amount of clumsy slaying
for God
was a fairly blunt instrument

in those early chanted alphabets
you could wield him over others
like the moon   which after all
was one rough rock

but there were odder shapes   inside us
all the hustling   amorous chemicals
and all the water wondering
where the larger ocean went

and lonely

but still we were a sight
when photographed from space
that time

blue from rim to rim
and wisps of feathery white
like brushstrokes
flicked from a quick
deft wrist

it was a work of art almost
to rise enough to see the shape
it wasn't just the photograph

the art was in the rising
from a world   so minor
and lovely
among all the major dark

so blue it almost hurt
to hurt another   like God repenting
those early bouts of wrath

still willing to learn
beyond which there's nothing
greater

for how could one so love
the world   or a universe
be worth its salt
if not mortal

how could matter   matter
without the yearning
and failing   but
nevertheless finding

something almost too big
to feel   in the blue curves
of this world
and the torn clouds

and the darkness all around

such elbow room
to give us space to spin
and somewhere
finally to go.

II

ORION SPUR

I like it here, just above the elbow of the out-flung arm
of the galaxy. I like the way objects retain the history
of motion in their shapes, and things that aren't
still appear. *Make yourself useful* my grandfather said,
handing me a hoe or hammer or spool of jute
to tie up the tomato vines. I like the tentacled way
the galaxy flowers and spins and how dust catches
your eye when lit and far away. You feel the weight
at the center like a negative sun, or the immense
concentration of God. Everything wants inward
but the wanting whirls it outward like when funnels
of dirt rose and twisted across the drought struck fields.

Make yourself useful, he'd say. I'd unwind the hose
and drag it between furrows, then moan and complaint
from the engine in the pump house would commence
and the sprinklers spin and the water shine like the soul
of the well released, then evening back when stars
were still visible, though some weren't stars at all,
I know now, but galaxies themselves, or clusters of galaxies,
or super-clusters, but what I remember was how the fronds
of new shoots rose and climbed the next day and now even
fifty years later the smell of tomato leaves if I rub them
is my grandfather in motion among dust and stars made useful.

HEAVEN

My grandfather wore a sweat stained fedora,
a red feather from a bantam rooster in the band,
and the mule he commanded seemed not so much
attached to the plow as *arrayed* in leather and hemp,
intersecting rings, halter, belly band, and blinder,
and nebular swarms of sweat bee, horse fly, bottle fly,
and gnats like live particles of penance he hosted
for the curse of being a mule. My grandfather believed
work was the surest way to navigate time,
and time, though high and mighty any given day,
though flashed out in sun or expensive as rain,
all came down to dirt in the end, and you plowed
time, or your part of time, and planted and prayed,
but not with words you'd hear in church,
and no more to God than the mule prayed to God,
and no more toward heaven than the end of the row—
grain in the bucket, cold water from the well.

CHESTERFIELD

To speak with the eloquence of my Uncle Ed,
who lived that part of the war no one talked about
when they returned because so many didn't, who

would spin his not-quite-true quail hunting stories,
the slightly larger than possible coveys of bobwhites
flushed up from the stubbled fields near the atom

plant, to wave words like he waved the burning
wand of his Chesterfield, the small lit coal
of the story, and the signatures of smoke, tilt

of ash that seemed always about to fall, but always
a little more delay in the story—a lone bird
unaccounted for, a dog with supernatural instinct

pinned to the faint scent of the mystical covey,
one culvert further, one field and barbed wire fence
beyond, and then a quick draw from the cigarette, the ash

tapped into the pants cuff, the lie descending like mercy
upon those of us who had only seen movies of war,
hauled home those soaring orchestrations in our hearts.

I remember the spell the quail hunt spun for us, how
Uncle Ed felled those fabled birds in flight, for ill or good,
and told us what he couldn't, tucked into what he could.

GHOST ARMY

for an exhibit of prints by Ellsworth Kelly
(member of 23rd Headquarters Special Troops, 1943–44)

If art is a form of camouflage, subtle maneuvers
into the surfaces of the seen, these prints, for instance,
mostly abstract, beneath which lie certain impulses
embodied by technique, beneath which lies not
exactly an idea, more an old inclination
sprung from the itch of common mortality,
felt as if residing in each of us alone,

no wonder Kelly distilled the nature of things in frag-
mented bursts of color, line, surrounding space,
condensations of what's too vast and blank to bear.

No wonder they drafted those art school students in 1943—
Ellsworth Kelly, Bill Blass, and the others—the *Ghost Army*,
they were called, to fabricate regiments of inflatable tanks,
fake cannons, rubber jeeps to outfox the Germans—Macy's style
weaponry they paraded across France.

No wonder all the hours broadcasting babble and static,
apparitional advances, retreats, whimsical alarms
riding the monitored airwaves.

If we can occupy the enemy with killing what's *not*
might a little more of what *is* survive?

Phantom platoons bobbing along the French hedgerows.
Decoy convoys floating towards the Rhine, seeming
to come from everywhere, or possibly nowhere?

It's surprising the Germans never caught on, maybe
counterattacked with their own imaginary forces, shelled
our synthetic soldiers with volleys of implied ordnance.
What if both sides began to just *make up* their weapons,
then started conjuring their motives as well
right down to the very notion of nation?

Why not fabricate not just the reason to die,
but the death itself?

If we pretend our slaughters on a broad enough scale,
and the others acquiesce, planting picturesque rows
of white crosses on graves filled with, I don't know—
sawdust effigies, expertly shrouded bales of straw,
could the Ghost Army come back to save us still?

Might the fake offensive, the wily bombardments
of sound and fury allow the rest of us to just—
stay home? Could the next war wage itself
and the mock armies win or lose, for all we care?

Can we be sufficiently occupied by artifice?

Though most of the Ghost Army is gone, or near the brink
of their actual graves by now, I want to call them back
to launch a last offensive. I want the enemy, foreign
and domestic, inside my heart and head, and out,
to feign falling down in their numbers, in meadows,
in histrionic billows of gun smoke over the gullies.

I want long winded consecrations and eulogies,
torrents of theatrical grieving on all sides. I want
somber enough art to commemorate the dead
so poignantly
they need not even bother to die.

Let the shapes and colors of the ritual
hide us under the clamor, alive and kicking.

If all art is subterfuge, let the dark demands of the moment
be appeased by invention and show, while we pause,
mere flesh and bone, in the shelter of the ordinary,
on common streets, on winter nights, let's say,
browsing the stores still open, milling about in museums
for the most frivolous of reasons. *Look*—

here's a stroke of yellow, an abstract slant of green
to ponder, a red rhomboid, a spectral set of squares.
Here's what appears to be a cluster of oranges. And here
is a drawing of locust leaves—I remember those trees
from childhood—early summer, bees
swarming the flower studded branches,
how you could stand beneath the blossoms
and be filled with the humming yourself.

If the essence of an image is the motion inside,
the live orbital wonder of particle and wave
that holds each print precisely in place,
no wonder what moves in memory now
is the scent and hum of the locust trees, the smoke
with which we bewildered the bees and robbed
their hives of honey, how the sweetness
seemed more than itself, as if each drop
held the flowers and the thorns and the smoke
and even the seasons still to come.

Though *sweetness* is not quite word enough,
and time is not quite long enough to tell
how it truly tasted, melting into the tongue
and into the body and years until now. *Look*—

here are some pictures pinned to the wall, a wedge
of green, a cluster of oranges, a print of locust leaves.
Here is the milling about, the buzz and ghostly
echo of gallery talk, the sweet diversions
of ordinary evening, behind which looms not
exactly an idea, more an old inclination to linger
and look, let the senses bleed out into the bright
shared surfaces, while we pause, mere flesh and bone,
deep in the mortal wonder, harbored in the artifice
of each of us alone.

THE BEES

And so it came to pass I knew little by little
less than before, and before knew less of me.
All the grasses burned the same green as ever
and the planets completed their rounds, but
motion wore me almost out, like a favorite
shirt. Not that *style* was ever that much *into* me.
Songs I loved grew blatantly passé, and loves
I loved were old ladies in the eyes of others.
Common mirrors lied straight to my face.
The very seasons grew dismissive. Perfect windfalls
of pollen were routed increasingly elsewhere.
Their lovely, minute addresses blurred as I tried
to read them on the wing, breath by breath.
It's all in the hands of the bees now, I thought,
but the bees, poor dears, were counting on *me*,
having all but forgotten their dances.

HOLLYHOCKS

The hollyhocks regulated the bees
all up and down the fence line.

They were spoken by God
according to the Bible. Let there be this.

Let there be that. Great whales. Strings of stars
to mark the enveloping seasons. Hollyhocks.

They were sung from the slow white mouth of the sun,
strung or strewn high as a man,

but the flowers—deep, fluid, flared out like cake ornaments,
or the bells of small colorful churches

from June to frost. Stunned bells then.
Stilled tongues. Dry stalks of pink and yellow torches

sapped of buzz and fire, lashed to the wire fence,
as the Bible foretold—wind laced, wanting to lean,

until somebody noticed, on the way to the hayfield,
and more or less mowed them out of mercy.

GREEN DAY

The string bean white kid
head-bangs to Green Day
in the cab of the tractor.

Corn dust rises and floats
over the interstate, a gold
horizon. He'll never admit

to loving this band, since
he's pretty sure they're over,
but the blur of chords

and the repetition, the drive
of the once cool singer
before he went blond and political

is like the John Deere itself
hammered down, the fuzz
of dust over the rented land,

and the girl his heart races to
at school, who'll leave for college,
he knows, and learn the names

of bands too real to record,
too cutting edge to even form.
He cranks the volume louder.

He's pretty sure he's losing
his hearing, but wants to feel
the bones vibrate, his skull

expand, as he swings the chute
and lets it blast, and chops
the world he knows to silage.

NIGHTLY NEWS

My own beheading was more gradual, each day advanced
a little, each evening a little wine to staunch the worry. I fingered
the stem of the glass, as if re-fashioning the moment,
but a little looser was my head at every turning of the stem.

Time is a dull machete, they say. No they don't. Nevertheless,
my head, this goblet of dread, this bauble of glitter not profound
grew loose. The mortal project of my life, the quelling of radiance,
edged closer and closer to completion. My mind, such a bother
when left to its own devices, received the nightly news like scarves

from the pockets of clowns. So much distant hurt to learn.
My part?—to cringe and buy, remotely condemn, accommodate
the cauldron of distant voices, losses and loomings, and at best,
throw flowers of concern at this or that, while the screens flashed
and the impending filled the living room like ocean swells.

The more channels I flicked the more my head rose lightly,
lifted and fluttered, filled with the bright vapors of what I saw
and heard merely for the nightly sake of the severing?
It takes time for the tissues to part, the cord to uncouple.
Nevertheless, there is my head unmistakable in the masked

man's hand. I am free to fall back into the remnant body now,
slow terror I became myself. I remember the weight of sorrow
lifted, and wondered if it was better, braver, to watch and know,
or to turn away was kindness, or was it too much to ask of myself
to be the head and blade and assassin, as well as the turning away?

GET RIGHT WITH GOD

the sign in the soybeans said,
white boards lettered in a shade of red
you sometimes see at murder sites.
It wasn't an invitation.

On the other hand, goldenrod
shook along the roadside.
Barbed wire sagged like the swaybacked
horses it held in the field.

Swing low, I thought as I drove,
but that was just a song.
I wasn't ready, or right
with any god who might
come to carry me.

I just drove the county roads
reading scripture from the barn sides,
wondering how the larks
chose where to land, which rain-
grooved post or stretch of wire
resembled home enough to sing.

I CALL YOUR NAME

Have a good day the gas attendant says.
She's moved on by the time I wish her
the same. I walk between the pumps,
unlock the door, and driving the hideous
beltline, remember one. In the back seat
with Donny, seventh grade friend—
on the way home from church with his parents
we sang most of the *Beatles' Second Album*.
He had the range of an angel, higher than Paul.
Ten years later Donny handed me a white tab
at a party. I was too shy to refuse
or even ask. I split it with my date. There was
a stray dog on the lawn of the Newman Center
who specialized in comedy. He forgave us. Loved us
as if we were not human. I'd never noticed
what they can do with their brows, the signs
and cosigns. There was something about time,
how full of what we mostly filter out, time is,
how little of a given instant we inhabit.
After Donny left prison the second time
I saw him with his daughter in the choir
of Broadway Baptist—one of those barn sized
southern churches, the center aisle wide as the runway
where the Lord will land his comeback plane.
She had the same gumption, Donny's kid,
you could see it, the practiced posture, breath
from deep in the diaphragm. Later, in the solo,
I could hear the voice was handed down.
I never thanked Donny for wrecking
my brain. After the revelations, came
several hours of terror. But the part
about the dog, the beneficent face

and deep watery eyes, the glory
of the muzzle, and how complicated
a moment can be, how many facets,
how bright the night grass, once you
erase the future and hold stupidly still.
Never thanked him for that, or the day
riding home in his parents' car, *a good day*,
I think, the church service quickly erased,
his parents, proud, amiable props.
I managed the lead on "Devil in Her Heart,"
the easy cover they let George sing.
But Donny, belting the harmony, even then
could wail, years before they locked him up,
and years before they let him out
to teach his daughter intonation,
projection, and how to finally let it fly,
and decades before I called up the woman
who'd split the tab with me.
It was cool, she remembered. Her own son
had just graduated. Her husband
was a writer, too. *There wasn't any dog*,
she said. *But it was cool.*

WHEN I THINK OF YOU I THINK OF HER

When I think of you I'm back in that silver room
with the sheet of Mylar taped to the wall by the bed.
Valentine's Day. How we swam in the ripples of wavy
reflection like two better people. Like looking into water.
There was upsy-daisy. There was minor tumbling,
shiny human tangles. The more the Scotch tape loosened,
the more the Mylar slacked and sagged, the more warped
the lovers got, no longer us, more fun than us, less fumbling,
more fluid. *They invented this in space*, the naked man in Mylar
said. *Good*, the rising woman said, kicking sheets away
which fell like ocean surf, and later small lappings
at the shore, and then, a little ashamed, in the waning novelty
of looking, in love's distorted aftermath, weightless now,
no more to do with us, the lovers closed their silver eyes
and floated out of sight.

STAY

The extravagance of the given moment
looped itself around us
like a glittery noose, or maybe some pearls,
or the blind ellipse of electrons
zooming through nowhere
for the sake of the timely nugget of *is*
at the center. *Stay,*
I said, to the clock and calendars.
I was talking to her, of course, and love,
and knew, the way one knows in time
the well-tiered knot of a noose,

the bee of elsewhere was in her bonnet,
and *honey this* and *honey that*
would not a melding make. *Love,*
I said, my hands loping the hills of her,
but small spring winds were on the move,
all flowers in a hurry.
And I will miss her through my days
though we walk the seasons down,
and sleep together tight as spoons,
and wear our rings like water
wears the likeness of a face.

SPRING SNOW

I guess the snow must love us deeply.
Smack in the heart of April the sharp
flakes fall. The branches can't catch them.
The snow plows grow sullen. The warblers
are stalled six hundred miles to the south, waiting
for rumors of green in the wind. Half of the waters
here are open. Half are a white waste where mallards
brood and crows rehash their guttural alphabets.

The snow must believe there's never enough.
Whatever we lack the sky can deliver? Loving
not wisely but a little too well, snow pierces
the air like so many pale tattoos
you can't remember why you coveted
such flakes as a child. Held out your arms.
Unfurled your tongue. Now all you remember
is the bite of spring snow falling out of love, I guess.

III

SEARCH COMMITTEE

You can sit anywhere, or even stand
if for some reason you're unable to sit
or offended by chairs, or faith
commands that you lie prone
or kneel in the presence of others,
or perhaps hover gently
during our interview? Anyway,
given your credentials and the flame
we've noticed tearing across your face,
we'd like to know we've made you
welcome. *Good.*

Now about those gaps in the résumé
and the need expressed in the flagrant
cut of your jacket, can you account
for your actions between nightfall
and bloody dawn? Were you

lost in a pit? Imprisoned
among the leaves?
What salaries were you hoarding
and how will this contribute
to the riches we've imagined
for ourselves? Did you love
your neighbor much?
Can you type? After sex
do you feel buoyant, or betrayed
by your demeanor?

Would you be more comfortable if we rose
and hovered with you now? Do you
function well among the living?
Would you like some spring water?

Has the bone-yard got your number?
If you could rearrange us in any way
so that we might function
as say, the river does, all glittery
and bright, and yet nobody's fool
what with the grinding down
into the canyons and all . . .

We've noticed you're weeping.
Would you leave it at that? Are there
questions about this position?

If you asked us for bread
and we offered a stone,
if you needed help
but our need was greater
would that be a problem?

We sense hesitancy on your part.
Perhaps you've read our minds—
Fly away from here
Fly away from here.

Frankly, we may have already
filled this position. Our memories
aren't perfect. But if we wanted to reach you
for any reason, say a trek
into the hinterlands, would currency
be required? Some other form of sacrifice?

You'll be hearing from someone soon
about something. We'd like to say
it's been a pleasure. It's strange
up here near the ceiling, isn't it? Look
how our neckties and shoelaces dangle.

RECEPTION

What I was thinking while you were talking
Where I was looking as you kept saying
What I was praying as time was passing
How time kept blinking in need of tending
As I was scanning the room for others
When talk exceeded the strength of smiling
As I was hoisted on the wave of one word
After another, nailed syllable by syllable
To the high holy branches beyond boredom
How back in childhood I pictured heaven
As seasons of nothing but decent behavior
As breath was dwindling, as light grew gray
As the party wore down like rivers will
Into the bedrock where the fossils of ancestors
Began to regret having persevered at all,
Slouching forward from sloughs
And brackish backwaters into what
You still had not finished saying
As the hours froze with rust and worlds
Wilted in the clusters of nearby galaxies
As I was wondering if there were saints
Of listening, and if I remained a little longer
Might others be saved, would reservoirs of silence
In the hearts and heads of the innocent
Be my gift and consolation, my water into wine
Though *I* might thirst, and time might bleed
If I threw my whole attention upon all
You were saying, like a body on a grenade
If I listened that others might not,
If I bore the brunt of all you unceasingly uttered
And likewise followed the gestures, batted my lashes
That the event, by which I mean life, might not perish,

If I became ashes on the altar of all you announced
Might I rise on some fair wind and circle the world
And find as I look down orbit after orbit
Upon what you had still not remotely ceased to say,
Would my life have been not quite in vain,
As I angeled above this bead, this bauble,
This frail blue world, could there be, quite frankly
A greater love than how I listened, though mortal,
to all you were saying?

JESUS JOGS

He runs through the clatter of shore birds.
The black-backed gulls rise. Plovers and turnstones
race like cops in silent movies he knows someday
will be invented. Lloyd Sterling is already his favorite.
He prays a pace to match the waves.

The lungs are buoyant, wing-like. The nerves
fire like nebulae, the muscles limber as time.
And what of the holy hamstrings?—such give
and take you would not believe
as the light switches on and off in the willows.

His disciples trail politely
like the Secret Service will someday lag
behind the American President,
feigning breathlessness.

But now the Lord unlatches his sandals
at the water's edge. And now
is something new.

The first mile on the sea the mind is clean.
The second, the way gets narrow.
And the third mile, feet now out past
all foam and whitecap, the faithful
shrunk to silhouettes on the shore,
the third mile
is nobody's business.

Has the Holy Ghost so flooded the cells,
he's just too wet to sink?

Is that even him out on the water?
Maybe a heron? Petrel, or gannet?

The faithful have multiplied by now,
clustered ankle deep in surf.

And now the sprint back home
is wave and absence, probability,
foretaste of science, leap of faith

as the Lord's robe flies with nobody in it
or so it seems from where we stand
and catch our breath, inventing a love
to fill, to keep this thing aloft.

IF YOU REALLY HAD TO

Would you, or not? If the chance
afforded itself? If some effort were required?
Whereas others might balk, would you?

If it presented itself? Knocked and just stood there?
Rustled timidly in the underbrush? Would you
if commanded by a dream?

If a god were watching, with no inclination
to bless or condemn? If it were remotely
possible? If it might come to nothing?

If you had the time? If it weren't for the stigma?
If on an island? Under the gun? If wishes
were horses? Would you, or not?

If flames were involved, but only a few?
If nimble enough? Or needled a little?
If you had to answer now? If you really had to?

HAPPINESS

The storm was headed in our direction—
big loom of gray like the absolute West
leaned over us. Reports of damage
in the neighboring counties—a silo unfurled
and took wing, a house trailer
twisted loose. On the Doppler screen
the storm looked alive, yellow and green
at the fringes, with a fierce red heart
trending to violet. Sirens swept over
to scare it away, like songbirds
grow strident, circle and bluff
at the sight of an owl.
When the rain came in sheets,
I regretted my sins. When lightning
cracked the red pine's half-rotted heart,
I wished the world more joy
in general. When the worst was over
and the grass lay flat, but alive,
and the sky was a waning bruise,
I thought of that silo, how it wasn't mine,
and all that grain cast back into the world's
wind, maybe some of it still flying.

TUPELO

Once, in love, which I consider to be a place
like France or Tupelo, Mississippi, I sat
on a swing on the porch of the house where Elvis
was born. It was late in the century and evening.
The house was closed. No one but us, and the cicadas
in the trees—a strange wave of sound amplified
by darkness, composed of moving parts, but still
a single wave up from the ground, having climbed
the grooves of bark, having shed their outer bodies,
the cicadas sang from what's left after the body, I think,
does the long dark work of repair. Ours wasn't a romance
destined to survive. I knew that as we stood
over the ditches where they pitched the Confederate
dead at Shiloh. There was a lizard on a rail fence
with a better chance of lasting love
than we had. A few months later lots of tears
and seized air in the phone lines,
all the mortal opera one might imagine
as the little boat of woe rocked between us,
and well, the less said about wonder
gone to waste, the better.
                            But back to the swing
and rhythm of that late summer evening,
the cicadas in the branches over the porch,
and later the motel, the map one lover makes
of another. That's how I remember Tupelo,
the flower of which makes a decent honey. If time
carved love's epitaph from one particular evening,
I'd pick that swing on Elvis's porch.
                            He had a twin, you know,
who died at birth, and therefore the hitch
in his early voice, the *thanatos* tearing through

the shotgun shack holy racket of those early Sun records,
as if the one who leaves is always there
in the trees, in the voice, in the rust of the chains
of the swing, in the spoon in the honey. That's why music
breaks your heart just to mend it, and vice versa,
and why, if love is a place you can't quite go back to,
still a few times already in this very memory
I've felt the tug of those chains, heard the voice
of the angel brother who haunted Elvis down,
and tasted something sharp and sweet.

AFTER LEAVING *THE POETICS OF SPACE* ON A CHAIR ON THE DECK ALL NIGHT

Some books are too beautiful to read.
You carry them around like a crush,
crave something in the loops and glamour
of sentences you're not sure
you're meant to possess. Whatever
in the language expands like space
actual reading seems to puncture.

Can this be true? You carry such books.
Press leaves into them. A piece of clover.
Start them. Put them down. Reread
and underline the terrifying parts,
which strangely makes you happy.

To read poetry is essentially to daydream,
Gaston Bachelard writes, the most serious
way to live. All night the dog-eared book
lay on the back deck under a coffee cup,
under starlight, a blunt bit of moon,
not glossy, nor bright enough to spellbind.

As though imagination created a nerve fiber,
is how Bachelard describes the movement
of an image into a line. But my favorite part
is how it lay on the deck all night, how wet
it was this morning, the round brown stain
on the cover. How it occupied only
its rightful share of space and time,
and yet I slept in my bed like a saint,

as if the house were blessed by paragraphs,
whole chapters I could wake this morning
and still not read. *Reverberation*
is what the poem sets in motion in the past,
or maybe it's the other way around, or maybe
I'm remembering ahead of time the parts
I still intend to read. Such a book *should be*
left out in the dew. How wise I felt to find it there.

THE WORLD AS YOU SAW IT

for William Stafford

Now that you're tucked in time's fold,
gravity's pocket, and the rabbit-quick
thought is back in the hat, now that
words are where you live, lines
like stones rolled away, where the tomb
is empty if the story makes it so, now
that the cameras can't find you,
and you've vanished from phone books,
it's just poetry, isn't it, the afterlife?

But no less real for being imagined.
For *being*, imagined, *is* the world
as you saw it, river and swallow flight,
hometown and tamarack, and once seen
like that, it's a different world; a richer
shade of yellow shakes the aspens like God,
and the leaves grow loud and so expensive
even the wind can't spend them all, even
the poem is small change by comparison.

THE WREN

What was the wren to me? A small stray volt
in the shrubbery. A song made of ticking
escaped from the clock.

What was the sparrow? From the dust bath
will rise a better dust, sang the sparrow,
as she lowered the standards of beauty
that all might enter, even

the strangest bird, the self. What was the crow?
When the raven wakes up, and it's only day,
in an average town, hackberries and pines,
no poetry or carrion, no glamour but the sheen
left over on the wings, residue of the raven
is the crow.

What was the swift, or the swallow? The air
churns live as the ocean. So reads the swerving,
the loop and arc of swallows. The not-so-secret
secret of constant flight
is hunger.

What was the self? Not in the bird book,
not in the branches. Made of the wren
and risen dust moved to wonder.

Not at the feeder, not
on the wing. What happens to be
in search of a habit. Not in the book.
Some kind of song.

SNOWFLAKE

Borrowing from snow before anyone
plants a boot print down, the page this morning
is a winter of its own,
over the reaches of which I might say
what I wish I knew.

I wish I knew you, for instance.
I wish I knew the long run
of love. If it ended well, or at all.

Where does the long run start kicking in,
by the way? Beyond which stark set of trees
or warehouses, or staggered
quartet of silos? Where on the calendar
do you dash down a finger and say—*there,*

that's the day we are happy, or hopeless,
or hapless, I'm afraid?

Dart a finger down and say—*this*
is the sum of two people together,
the way it will be written
and henceforth understood.

Henceforth—I borrow this word
from the ornate
trappings of precision.

The long run has ruined my life,
I think. I borrow this thought
from the snow that stretches today
across the valleys and onto the flatlands
beyond the river.

I wish I could walk there
into the still falling snow.

Or not want to know you
beyond the moment at hand,
the falling one, the single flake
they say is intricate
and unrepeatable.

CHICKADEES

Those lapses in the heartbeat, fumblings
in the rhythm, like when the bassist
has had too many beers and you have to wait
till he flags the drummer down again.
Still, it's music. Still, it's unsettling
to feel the heart give ground, go even
a few beats wrong. The breath gets hilly
and you miss like a hometown
the reliable rise and dip, rise and dip.
The way chickadees fly—it's like that,
no straight line, but a willful rippling
carries them into the lower branches
of the linden where the best shadows lie.
Chickadees weigh the same as a stack of three dimes,
I've read. Lower their heart rates
to something beyond ghostly in winter.
They're dead, essentially,
some snowy nights in the trees.
And then comes day, light bouncing
off the snow, resurrecting hunger.
I think about the chickadees,
how good it is they don't die long,
when my own heart wobbles
and breath begins to guess,
snagging oxygen on the wing
instead of just letting it come
like the resolving note in a major key
or the wind small birds ride home.

HOME

Here's to the bale of oats, badly strung,
a little escaping on the way to the barn
for the sparrows to weave into the rafters.

And the whim of the mare as she races the colt
for no reason we need to know. Here's to the vortex
of pigeon wings winding to roost on the slopes
of the silo. The clucking and preening.

And here's to the day of the weevil
climbing back into the light of the world
all those months infused for him, all that
wet lowdown waiting for the Lord
to reopen the gates of the ground.

Here's to the manner in which it comes
and goes, or came and went, or hangs like smoke
over the field burned off for plowing
some windless day in the mind.

BLINK

They're passing plates to me. *Growing boy*,
they say. Bright stacks of corn like golden scrolls
fresh from the typewriters of angels.

It's good to be somebody's child. Blessed
are the little ones—the mote, the dingy sparrow.
For they shall sing and fill the hole in the heart,

or maybe it's doves and the soul? They're passing platters
of potatoes and beans in the Methodist basement,
ham on the bone. And greens that resemble sea sludge,

dark and ancient. The preacher says the blessing.
His tie is loose. His belt undone. It's down to business
now the sermon's over. A spoon stands up in gravy.

Pats of butter like bricks for the heart's yellow houses.
Pickles smell like battery acid; strict and scientific
is how all vinegar seems to me.

They're passing cornbread now. They're passing plenty.
Already summer outside, but cool and damp
in the basement and the long unfolded tables

covered with not-quite-matching cloths.
Glasses of iced tea ring like bells or money.
The Methodist men roll up their sleeves.

The women's aprons are untied, folded and stacked.
When Jesus rose they found the shroud like that.
Never leave a mess.

They're passing chicken—fried, fricasseed.
I knew these hens back home, the sunlight
on their feathers as they fussed at the dirt,

drilled and scratched under the mimosa.
Like a perfumed broom it swept the ground.
A company of minor angels, is how they seemed.

We wrung their necks, my grandmother did.
Dust to dust. Bible lessons on the basement walls.
Moses and the burning bush. Peter with his fishing nets.

Above us now, the sanctuary empty
as the ark unloaded. And we're down here
in something's belly, like Jonah,

who might have seen through the great whale's eyes
where he was going. Maybe xylophone the ribcage
to make the big fish let him out?

This is my blood and this is my body,
the preacher said as we knelt up there.
Daylight butchered out the window.

They pass more plates and platters to me. *Growing boy*,
they say again. Food so fat and good I hurt all over. Meringue
is how I picture the roofs of the mansions in heaven.

And now we're climbing into light. *Blink*
into the midday sun. And now the car door slamming.
And the engine's great authority.

Blink and we're already down the road.
The plates are dried, and put away. And the hands
that held them under the sun. All that's folded up in time.

Such things they passed to me. Sweet milk
to wash the cobbler down. *Growing boy*
like you, they said, *can surely hold a little more.*

THE BEST THINGS IN LIFE
ARE THE MOST EXPENSIVE

Grass for instance which shines with the wet light of morning
and lines the bottoms of small baskets and valleys costing
all the way from the center of the sun, photons
pin-balling their way to the unfurling corona and then

smack into the sheen on the face of the grass. And kissing
which costs approximately a fortune in stirred-up chemistry
and repercussions, betrayals and strollers and sonnetry
and then all those shopping days until remorse is done.

And snowfall which is the bread of heaven though broken
by the time it gets here, but lovely when wind carved
and shattered into spectral bits by low angles of light.
And then training the pine branches to balance the snow.

All expensive. And music which took millions of years of birds
and wolves and longing to learn. And true love which costs
an arm and a leg in imagination alone, not to mention the sexual
appliances like cars and shoes and well-appointed lairs.

And words that well up and want to be but nerve is missing
and must be hunted up and down the corridors of the spine
separated out from the more plentiful cut-rate words
that shine a little, but soon wreck or stick or cease to console.

So expensive, hardly less than unaffordable are the best things—
time and memory and forgetting, water wearing over rocks
that took half the life of the planet to form, and wishing
you could hear it more deeply and longer and also silence.

WISCONSIN POETRY SERIES
Ronald Wallace, *Series Editor*

New Jersey (B) • Betsy Andrews

Salt (B) • Renée Ashley

Horizon Note (B) • Robin Behn

About Crows (FP) • Craig Blais

Mrs. Dumpty (FP) • Chana Bloch

The Declarable Future (4L) • Jennifer Boyden

The Mouths of Grazing Things (B) • Jennifer Boyden

Help Is on the Way (4L) • John Brehm

Sea of Faith (B) • John Brehm

Reunion (FP) • Fleda Brown

Brief Landing on the Earth's Surface (B) • Juanita Brunk

Ejo: Poems, Rwanda, 1991–1994 (FP) • Derick Burleson

Jagged with Love (B) • Susanna Childress

Almost Nothing to Be Scared Of (4L) • David Clewell

The Low End of Higher Things • David Clewell

Now We're Getting Somewhere (FP) • David Clewell

Taken Somehow by Surprise (4L) • David Clewell

Borrowed Dress (FP) • Cathy Colman

Places/Everyone (B) • Jim Daniels

Show and Tell • Jim Daniels

Darkroom (B) • Jazzy Danziger

And Her Soul Out of Nothing (B) • Olena Kalytiak Davis

My Favorite Tyrants (B) • Joanne Diaz

Talking to Strangers (B) • Patricia Dobler

Immortality (4L) • Alan Feldman

A Sail to Great Island (FP) • Alan Feldman

The Word We Used for It (B) • Max Garland

A Field Guide to the Heavens (B) • Frank X. Gaspar

The Royal Baker's Daughter (FP) • Barbara Goldberg

(B) = Winner of the Brittingham Prize in Poetry

(FP) = Winner of the Felix Pollak Prize in Poetry

(4L) = Winner of the Four Lakes Prize in Poetry

Funny (FP) • Jennifer Michael Hecht

The Legend of Light (FP) • Bob Hicok

Sweet Ruin (B) • Tony Hoagland

Partially Excited States (FP) • Charles Hood

Ripe (FP) • Roy Jacobstein

Saving the Young Men of Vienna (B) • David Kirby

Falling Brick Kills Local Man (FP) • Mark Kraushaar

Last Seen (FP) • Jacqueline Jones LaMon

The Lightning That Strikes the Neighbors' House (FP) • Nick Lantz

You, Beast (B) • Nick Lantz

The Unbeliever (B) • Lisa Lewis

Slow Joy (B) • Stephanie Marlis

Acts of Contortion (B) • Anna George Meek

Bardo (B) • Suzanne Paola

Meditations on Rising and Falling (B) • Philip Pardi

Old and New Testaments (B) • Lynn Powell

Season of the Second Thought (FP) • Lynn Powell

A Path between Houses (B) • Greg Rappleye

The Book of Hulga (FP) • Rita Mae Reese

Don't Explain (FP) • Betsy Sholl

Late Psalm • Betsy Sholl

Otherwise Unseeable (4L) • Betsy Sholl

Blood Work (FP) • Matthew Siegel

The Year We Studied Women (FP) • Bruce Snider

Bird Skin Coat (B) • Angela Sorby

The Sleeve Waves (FP) • Angela Sorby

Wait (B) • Alison Stine

Hive (B) • Christina Stoddard

The Red Virgin: A Poem of Simone Weil (B) • Stephanie Strickland

The Room Where I Was Born (B) • Brian Teare

Fragments in Us: Recent and Earlier Poems (FP) • Dennis Trudell

The Apollonia Poems (4L) • Judith Vollmer

Level Green (B) • Judith Vollmer

Reactor • Judith Vollmer

Voodoo Inverso (FP) • Mark Wagenaar

Hot Popsicles • Charles Harper Webb

Liver (FP) • Charles Harper Webb

The Blue Hour (B) • Jennifer Whitaker

Centaur (B) • Greg Wrenn

Pocket Sundial (B) • Lisa Zeidner